ALABAMA ILLUSTRATED
ENGRAVINGS FROM 19TH CENTURY NEWSPAPERS

TEXT AND CAPTIONS BY
JAMES L. BAGGETT AND KELSEY SCOUTEN BATES
IMAGES FROM THE BIRMINGHAM PUBLIC LIBRARY ARCHIVES

TURNER
PUBLISHING COMPANY

The Market, Mobile, Alabama
Harper's Weekly, July 16, 1887
Artist: Charles Graham

ALABAMA ILLUSTRATED
ENGRAVINGS FROM 19TH CENTURY NEWSPAPERS

Turner Publishing Company
www.turnerpublishing.com

Alabama Illustrated: Engravings from 19th Century Newspapers

Copyright © 2009 Turner Publishing Company

Library of Congress Control Number: 2009922662

ISBN-13: 978-1-59652-536-8

ISBN 978-1-68442-276-0 (hc)

CONTENTS

ACKNOWLEDGMENTS..VII

INTRODUCTION 1

THE SECEDING ALABAMA DELEGATION IN CONGRESS.................... 3

PORTRAIT OF HON. WILLIAM R. KING, VICE PRESIDENT OF THE UNITED STATES 4

RESIDENCE OF THE LATE VICE PRESIDENT KING—HIS DEATH PLACE 6

SCENE ON THE ALABAMA RIVER, LOADING COTTON............................ 8

THE TILT.. 10

THE AMPHITHEATRE 12

STATE HOUSE WHERE THE CONGRESS OF THE SOUTHERN CONFEDERACY MEETS 14

INAUGURATION OF PRESIDENT JEFFERSON DAVIS 16

COTTON-SHOOT ON THE ALABAMA AND SHOOTING COTTON-BALES 18

CITY OF MONTGOMERY, ALABAMA.. 20

THE CABINET OF THE CONFEDERATE STATES AT MONTGOMERY............ 22

THE WHITE HOUSE AT MONTGOMERY—RENT $5000 A YEAR 24

UNION SOUTHERN MEN WELCOMING OUR GUN-BOATS IN ALABAMA................ 26

THE CITY OF HUNTSVILLE, ALABAMA 28

SEARCHING FOR REBELS IN A CAVE IN ALABAMA 30

THE MURDER OF GENERAL ROBERT L. M'COOK, NEAR SALEM, ALABAMA 32

STEVENSON HELD BY UNION FORCES AND NEGROES BUILDING STOCKADES 34

THE WAR IN ALABAMA—FORT GRANT 36

STEVENSON, ALABAMA 38

HUNTSVILLE, ALABAMA, FROM GENERAL LOGAN'S HEAD-QUARTERS 40

Our Fleet off Mobile, View of Mobile, Grant's Pass, and Fort Morgan 42

Soldiers' Ball at Huntsville, Alabama—Dancing the "Virginia Reel" 44

Fort Morgan and the Rebel Fleet and Off Mobile 46

The Federal Army Crossing the Coosa River 48

Alabamians Receiving Rations 50

Pictures of the South—Magnolia Grove, on the Shell Road at Mobile 52

An Illegal Still in Alabama 54

View of the Tombigbee River, Alabama 56

Emerson College, Mobile, Alabama 58

Approach to Montgomery, Alabama 60

A Night Drill on the Levee at Mobile, Alabama 62

Mobile—The Gulf City 64

Szene nahe Leeds, Alabama, wahrend des Sturmes am 19, Februar 1884 66

Berherung des Sturmes in Alabama 68

The Camp Ground, The Grand Review, and The Prize Company 70

The New Bridge over the Alabama at Selma 72

Fiftieth Anniversary of the Montgomery True Blues 74

The Recent Floods in the Alabama River—A Family Refuge in a Tree-Top 76

Birmingham, Alabama—Scene in a Real Estate Exchange 78

The Great Industry of Birmingham, Alabama—A Pig Iron Furnace 80

Charcoal Burners 82

Coke Ovens 84

Wharf Scene at Mobile, Alabama 86

Montgomery, Alabama 88

The Attack on the Jail at Birmingham, Alabama 90

Alabama—Disastrous Wreck, Near Birmingham 92

Booker T. Washington 94

Notes on the Engravings 97

Suggestions for Additional Reading 99

ACKNOWLEDGMENTS

This volume, *Alabama Illustrated: Engravings from 19th Century Newspapers,* is the result of the cooperation and efforts of many individuals and organizations. It is with great thanks that we acknowledge the valuable contribution of the following for their generous support:

Don Veasey, Birmingham Public Library Archives

Yolanda Valentin, Birmingham Public Library Archives

Gigi Gowdy, Birmingham Public Library Archives

Sara Roberts Stokes, Birmingham Public Library

Graham Boettcher, Birmingham Museum of Art

Dan Brooks, Arlington Antebellum Home and Gardens

Frances Robb, Independent Scholar

Patti Olvey, Gorgas Library, University of Alabama

We also wish to acknowledge the continued support of the Birmingham Public Library Board:

Gwendolyn B. Welch, President
Nell Allen, Vice-President
Shanta' Craig-Owens, Parliamentarian
E. Bryding Adams
Thomas J. Adams, Jr.
Gwendolyn R. Amamoo
Lillie M. H. Fincher
Anthony Johnson
Samuel A. Rumore, Jr.
Dora Sims
Jimmie S. Williams

And special thanks to Larry P. Langford, Mayor of Birmingham.

The Surface Cut at the Morris Iron Mine at Redding Near Birmingham, Alabama
Harper's Weekly, September 27, 1890
Artist: unknown

INTRODUCTION

In the nineteenth century, many Americans received news and learned about the world beyond their own hometowns by reading illustrated newspapers. Prior to the 1890s, the technology did not exist to economically publish photographs in newspapers, so some publishers employed artists to draw and engrave images of places, events, and people. Many of these engraved illustrations, which accompanied news stories, poems, and short fiction, are impressive for their detail and artistic quality.

From the 1850s to the 1890s, more than 250 engraved images of Alabama were published in national and international illustrated newspapers. This book contains more than 40 of those illustrations from five nineteenth-century newspapers: *Harper's Weekly* and *Frank Leslie's Illustrated Newspaper,* both published in New York; *Ballou's Pictorial* and *Gleason's Pictorial Drawing-Room Companion,* both published in Boston; and *The Illustrated London News,* a British publication. *Harper's* and *Frank Leslie's* were the best-known and largest-circulating American papers. The papers competed with one another, and Frank Leslie boasted that he could publish an image of an event within two weeks of it happening.

The brief time between an event and the printing of an illustration required newspaper publishers to follow a multi-step process in creating the image. For this reason, newspaper engravings provide a valuable but imperfect view of the past. An artist in the field, sometimes visiting a city or town or following an army, would make a preliminary sketch and often add notes. Sometimes that artist would finish the drawing later from notes or memory, or it was completed by a different artist at the newspaper's offices. Other engravings were copied faithfully from photographs, while some were drawn from the artist's imagination based on eyewitness accounts or news reports.

Once the paper sketch was completed, another artist then copied the paper drawing in reverse onto an engraving plate, usually made of wood or copper. For wood engraving, artisans cut away the blank spaces with a knife or other tool, leaving a raised image. Wood plates worked well in the printing presses of the time, and one plate could be used to print thousands of images. For copper plates, an artist incised the image into the surface of the copper using a steel tool called a burin. For large or complex engravings, several engravers divided the printing block into sections with each working on a different part.

The images of Alabama included here are typical of those published for many places. They include portraits of political leaders, landscapes, cityscapes, and events such as storms, parades, sports, and work. Historians have noted a tendency among the nineteenth-century northeastern press to portray the South as backward, exotic, or at the least, not like the North. The reader will see some of that tendency here, but the reader will also find images and excerpts from articles that are neutral or complimentary. The illustrations are more often positive or romanticized, while the articles are more often negative or dismissive. For example, many illustrations showing African Americans are more realistic and respectful than the text in some of the articles accompanying the images.

Today, newspaper engravings are used by historians for documentation and illustration and by history buffs for decoration. The images, many of which are widely available because hundreds of thousands were printed, are affordable collectibles. The Birmingham Public Library's Department of Archives and Manuscripts collects Alabama illustrations, and all of the images in this book are drawn from that collection. The captions that accompany the images are taken verbatim from the original sources. Artists have been identified when possible. The original spellings and eccentricities of nineteenth-century grammar have been largely retained.

This book is published to accompany the Birmingham Public Library's exhibition, Alabama Illustrated, that began touring museums, archives, libraries, historic sites, and community art centers around the state in 2009. For more information on the exhibition, contact the authors at the Birmingham Public Library.

The Seceding Alabama
Delegation in Congress
Harper's Weekly, February 9, 1861
Artist: unknown

Portrait of Hon. William R. King, Vice President of the United States
Gleason's Pictorial Drawing-Room Companion, March 12, 1853
Artist: G. H. Hayes

William Rufus King was the thirteenth vice-president of the United States, serving under Franklin Pierce. Though King was originally from North Carolina, he moved to the territory that is now Dallas County, where he helped build and name the city of Selma. He served as the first U.S. senator from Alabama from 1819 to 1844 and was minister to France between 1844 and 1846. King was ill with tuberculosis when he was inaugurated as vice-president and had moved to Cuba on doctor's orders to be in a warm environment. He was the only vice-president to be inaugurated outside the country; and he died in April 1853, shortly after his inauguration, at his home in Dallas County. This portrait appeared as a full-page illustration, opposite a portrait of President Pierce.

From the accompanying article: "On pages 168 and 169, we present two admirable and very perfect likenesses of President Pierce and Vice President King. We could not give our readers at this time more appropriate pictures. They are, as will be perceived, bold, artistic, and finely executed; and when the reader remembers that he gets both these large original pictures for six cents, and at the same time an array of other valuable and interesting illustrations, not to mention the large amount of original reading matter, also furnished, from known and able authors, he will realize, what is now universally admitted, that the Pictorial is the cheapest paper in the world."

Residence of the Late Vice President King—His Death Place
Frank Leslie's Illustrated Newspaper, April 30, 1853
Artist: W. R. Miller

The Dallas County residence of William Rufus King is pictured here. It was passed on to his sister after his death, and it burned in the 1920s, never to be rebuilt.

From the accompanying article: "The old man has returned home, but to die. The steamer Fulton conveyed him from Havana, to Mobile, from whence he reached his house, in Alabama, on Sunday, 17th inst., and died on the evening of the following day, 18th April, aged sixty-eight years. The late residence of Vice President King is situated east of the Alabama River, in Dallas County, Alabama, five and a half miles from the city of Cahawba. It is in the most healthy section of the county, being upon a beautiful elevation, covered with chestnut trees, and surrounded by extensive levels of majestic pines. The name it bears is 'Chestnut Hill,' and was given it by King himself."

Scene on the Alabama River, Loading Cotton
Ballou's Pictorial, November 28, 1857
Artist: Mr. Killburn

To accompany a complimentary article about Alabama's natural resources, fertile land, and remarkable population growth, illustrators at *Ballou's Pictorial* presented a lively scene of men loading cotton onto a steamboat in antebellum Alabama. Cotton commerce was at its height in the 1850s, with 41,964 farms producing 225,771,600 pounds of cotton. In comparison, Alabama produced 199,815,000 pounds of cotton in 2008.

From the accompanying article: "Of cotton, as we remarked in a former article, the exuberant soil of Alabama yields more than any other member of our prosperous confederacy of States. But this, though the staple, is by no means the only valuable agricultural product of a State singularly blessed in fertility. Towards the north, the low mountains are deep in grass, affording abundant pasturage to numerous herds of cattle. The central portion of the State is occupied by fertile prairies, and the southern, though often sandy and inferior in productiveness, has many fertile alluvial bottoms, on which rice is grown. In Marengo and Greene counties there were formerly extensive cane-brakes, which are now nearly cleared, disclosing some of the very best land in the State. Sugar cane grows in the southwest neck, between Mobile Bay and the Mississippi."

The Tilt
Harper's Weekly, November 27, 1858
Artist: from a sketch by Nixon

The Fourth Annual Fair of the Alabama State Agricultural Society was held in Montgomery from November 1 through 6, 1858. Staged on the high grounds near the Alabama River, the fair drew the national press to Alabama, which was fostering a vibrant agricultural economy. Though it had been admitted to the Union in 1819—39 years earlier—Alabama's agricultural economy surged just before the Civil War.

Jousting exercises such as the one demonstrated in "The Tilt"—in which a jouster attempts to thrust a lance through a ring—were skill-building exercises and intended for performance. Though the article makes no mention of this particular spectacle, it is obvious from the crowd gathered that it was popular entertainment at the fair.

From the accompanying article: "There are characteristic points of difference between a show of this kind in the Northern, and such a display as we are now describing in the Southern States. In the former, distinctive prominence is given to those mechanical appliances which represent the interests of the mighty grain growing countries of the North and the imperial Northwest. . . . There are men from the sooty forge and the clanking anvil; men from the dusty flouring-mill and the odorous laboratory of some noted perfumer; men whose ears are daily stunned by the whirr of spindles and the clatter of looms, men who listen forever to the groaning of ponderous wheels and the incessant puffings of busy steam engines. . . . At a Southern Fair, on the contrary, the eye at once discerns the habits, tastes, and pursuits of a people wholly given to agricultural and pastoral employments. But few machines are on exhibition, and those relate exclusively to the interests of the farm and to the homely duties of the planter. Here is, perhaps, a corn-sheller and separator, and there is a bit of mechanical ingenuity applied to the grinding of corn and the crushing of the cob. Not only does the visitor discover at a glance that the tillage of the soil is the noble vocation of the sturdy and happy yeomanry around him, but he sees with equal readiness that the one great, engrossing, controlling idea is the growth and culture of cotton. . . . I see a fellow sedulously bent upon twirling a crank for an admiring crowd, and thrusting my spectacles through some cranny in the living wall, I find a man explaining how some cute Yankees, way in Varmount, is trying to 'do' the Alabama planter with a cotton-packing contrivance, full of wheels, and screws, and levers. Thus it is on every side; you see the enshrinement of the mighty staple in the central fane of this great, warm, throbbing, Southern heart."

The Amphitheatre
Harper's Weekly, November 27, 1858
Artist: from a sketch by Nixon

The amphitheater, illustrated here with large crowds gathered to view a parade of horses, was a central showplace at the fair used for exhibiting everything from livestock to agricultural machinery.

From the accompanying article: "In addition to a large number of well-arranged stalls for cattle, hogs, and horses, there is a finely graveled training course: a grand amphitheatre for the examination of stock, and for the exhibition of hippodromic performances; a commodious two-story edifice for the proper display of mechanical contrivances, as well, also, for the use of exhibitors in the department of the fine arts."

The City of Montgomery, Alabama, Showing the State House Where the Congress of the Southern Confederacy Meets on February 4, 1861
Harper's Weekly, **February 9, 1861**
Artist: unknown

As the first capital of the Confederate States, Montgomery attracted the interest of national newspapers in early 1861. This illustration demonstrates solid landscape technique and is possibly taken from the vantage point of the roof of a building looking up what is now Dexter Avenue. The view toward the statehouse draws the observer's eye from the foreground—where the procession of people ends—to the background, where the procession begins, and where a new national government would soon meet. The accompanying article does not refer to this image.

Inauguration of President Jefferson Davis of the Southern Confederacy, at Montgomery, Alabama, February 18, 1861
Harper's Weekly, March 9, 1861
Artist: unknown

Nineteenth-century printing presses were slow, and a weekly publication would not have been possible before the *Illustrated London News,* first published in 1842, developed a technique for moving the artist's sketch from paper to engraved wood block while the news was still current. After an artist drew the illustration onto a printing block, that block was divided into smaller blocks so that many hands could work on carving one illustration at one time. Once the engraving was complete, the blocks were reunited for printing. Sometimes, hastily rejoined blocks would leave seam lines in the printed engravings. The seam lines are evident in the sky of this illustration of the statehouse in Montgomery, though a magnifying glass might be needed to see them. Aided by this technique, circulation for some illustrated newspapers reached 100,000 and 200,000 each week.

From the accompanying article: "On page 157 we publish a picture of the Inauguration of President Davis . . . from a photograph obligingly placed at our disposal. . . . A lady who witnessed the scene thus writes to a friend in this city: 'The President is a pleasant-looking old gentleman, of about fifty years of age. . . . He took the oath amidst the deepest silence; and when he had raised his hand and his eyes to heaven and said, "So help me God," I think I never saw any scene so solemn and impressive. . . . The Vice President is a constant visitor at the house where I stay; he is very slight and delicate looking, has more the appearance of a dead man than a living one, until he begins to speak, when you forget entirely how ugly he is.'"

COTTON-SHOOT ON THE ALABAMA.

Cotton-Shoot on the Alabama
Shooting Cotton-Bales into the Fore Part of the River Steamer Magnolia
The Illustrated London News, May 4, 1861
Artist: F. Bellew

The Illustrated London News was the world's first illustrated weekly newspaper and, by the time this article was written, was nearly 20 years old. These images reflect the international success of Alabama's cotton industry. The transport of cotton outside U.S. borders must have been of interest to readers worldwide, because Alabama's cotton trade was a regular feature in national and international journals.

From the accompanying article: "Our Number of April 13 contained some Illustrations of the methods of conveying cotton in India to the ports of shipment; and we follow up . . . by giving this week two companion Engravings illustrating the singular manner in which cotton-bales are sometimes taken on board steam-boats in the Alabama River, in Alabama, one of the seven Southern Confederate States of America. On the Mississippi the bales are merely dragged and trundled over a plank on board ship. But on the Alabama, the banks of which are frequently high and steep, a more dashing style of embarkation is adopted. . . . Mr. F. Bellew, the gentleman to whom we are indebted for our illustrations, supplies the following particulars. . . . 'At a given signal from below a thousand-pound package of the staple was started at the top of the slide, two hundred and fifty feet perpendicular above the level of the water. Slowly it moved at first, but, gaining momentum as it proceeded, the pace quickened—quicker, quicker, quicker—till at last it fell like a thunderbolt on the deck, knocking the bales of the barricade in every direction.'"

City of Montgomery, Alabama
Harper's Weekly, June 1, 1861
Artist: Drawn by our Special Artist Traveling with W. H. Russell, LL.D.

This illustration—depicting African American slaves working along the banks of the Alabama River outside Montgomery—is known as a *genre scene.* Common in nineteenth-century print media, genre scenes were sometimes realistic in their depiction of everyday life, but many were stylized, dramatized, or romanticized. In this engraving, the benign view of slavery ignores the brutality of the system. But the image illustrates an important aspect of Southern history: the city in the background depends on the forced labor of the people in the foreground for its prosperity and physical existence. The accompanying article does not refer to this image.

The Cabinet of the Confederate States at Montgomery
Harper's Weekly, June 1, 1861
Artist: unknown

The members of the Jefferson Davis cabinet pictured here did not sit for this drawing as a group. The *Harper's* writer tells his readers that the image is a composite "from photographs made at Washington and at Montgomery." Rather than referring to the image as a group portrait, the writer calls it "a group of portraits." In fact, the artist who completed the engraving seems to have been wholly unfamiliar with Alabama, because he placed a fanciful palm tree outside the illustration's window.

Pictured from left to right are Judah P. Benjamin, Attorney General; Stephen Mallory, Secretary of the Navy; Christopher Memminger, Secretary of the Treasury; Alexander Stephens, Vice-President; LeRoy Pope Walker, Secretary of War; Jefferson Davis, President; John H. Reagan, Postmaster General; and Robert Toombs, Secretary of State. The accompanying article gives a brief biographical sketch of each Confederate cabinet member.

The White House at Montgomery—Rent $5000 a Year
Harper's Weekly, June 1, 1861
Artist: unknown

For the first few weeks of his administration, Jefferson Davis and his wife lived in Montgomery's Exchange Hotel. In mid-April 1861, the couple moved to the Italianate house pictured here. Built in 1835, the house belonged to a Montgomery lawyer and was rented for the "First Couple." Situated on the corner of Washington and Bibb streets, the house was an easy walk from the capitol and provided space for the Davises to host receptions. The accompanying article does not mention the house.

Union Southern Men Welcoming Our Gun-Boats in Alabama
Harper's Weekly, March 1, 1862
Artist: unknown

North Alabama had fewer slaves than the southern part of the state, and many in the north opposed secession. In 1860, some Unionists proposed forming a new state out of areas of Alabama, Tennessee, and Georgia that held Union sympathies. Alabama Unionists were a minority, but many served in the Union army, operated as spies for Federal forces, or fought as pro-Union guerrillas against Confederate irregulars.

From the accompanying article: "On this page we illustrate the Welcome of the Union men in Tennessee and Alabama to the gun-boats which ascended the Tennessee River. . . . During the night the gun-boats went to Florence, Alabama. . . . Everywhere along the river they were received with astonishing welcome by numerous Union families in Southern Tennessee and Northern Alabama, and at the towns along the river the old flag was looked upon as a redeemer, and hailed with loud shouts of joy. The people of Florence are so delighted at finding the Stars and Stripes once more giving protection to them that they were prepared to give a grand ball to the officers of the gun-boats, but the latter could not remain to accept their courtesies."

The City of Huntsville, Alabama
Harper's Weekly, August 2, 1862
Artist: unknown

Union forces occupied Huntsville on April 11, 1862, withdrew the same month that this illustration was published, and took the city again in July 1863.

From the accompanying article: "Huntsville was taken by General Mitchell some three months ago. It is a pretty town, the capital of Madison County; has a court-house, bank, quite a number of churches, and nearly 3000 inhabitants. . . . General Mitchell swooped down upon it one fine morning at daybreak, when the rebels hadn't an idea of his approach, frightening the people of the neighborhood so terribly that they haven't recovered since."

Searching for Rebels in a Cave in Alabama
Harper's Weekly, August 16, 1862
Artist: Mr. Hubner

Union forces operated in north Alabama throughout most of the Civil War and were frequently harassed and attacked by snipers, small bands of Confederate forces, and guerrillas.

From the accompanying article as described by the artist: "On our way from Bridgeport back to Huntsville two of our men got shot by some bushwhackers. . . . Colonel J. Beatty stopped the train and sent several detachments in pursuit of the rebels. One party went to the town and captured four or five of the band; another party . . . went into a cave. . . . A slave negro led the way. . . . We had to walk some distance with heads bent; but soon the cave got wider and wider, and looked like a church with fine columns and arches, strange formations of the dropping limestone. The red blaze of the torches produced a strange and beautiful effect. Often it seemed to us that we saw human figures in the deep shadow, often we raised our trusty rifles, but found we were aiming at some curious limestone formation. We went about two miles into the cave, found signs of occasional visits by human beings, and the negro assured us it was in fact a hiding-place of a guerrilla band."

The Murder of General Robert L. M'Cook, Near Salem, Alabama
Harper's Weekly, August 23, 1862
Artist: unknown

Robert McCook, an attorney, organized and trained the Ninth Ohio Infantry in Cincinnati. While serving as the unit's commander in northern Alabama, he fell ill with dysentery and was being transported by ambulance when killed by Confederate irregulars. An earlier image showed pro-Union Alabamians celebrating the arrival of Federal troops, but McCook's troops complained that other north Alabama whites applauded the death of their commander.

From the accompanying article: "On Tuesday last General Robert L. M'Cook, who was at the time very sick, was in an ambulance near Salem, Alabama, on his way to his brigade. The ambulance was traveling over the usual military road . . . . Before the ambulance had proceeded three miles the driver discovered that he was pursued by guerillas. . . . The guerrilla leader ordered the ambulance to stop. . . . The vehicle was then upset, and the sick officer turned into the road. While on his knees, helpless and sick, he was fired at by a ruffian, and shot through the side. . . . The Ninth Ohio, M'Cook's own regiment, on learning of the assassination, marched back to the scene of the occurrence, burned every house in the neighborhood and laid waste the lands. Several men who were implicated in the murder were taken out and hung to trees by the infuriated soldiery."

THE TOWN OF STEVENSON, ALABAMA, HELD BY THE UNION FORCES.—Sketched by Mr. H. Mosler.—[See Page 558.]

The Town of Stevenson, Alabama, Held by Union Forces
Negroes Building Stockades Under the Recent Act of Congress
Harper's Weekly, August 30, 1862
Artist: H. Mosler

The town of Stevenson, Alabama, is located in Jackson County near the Georgia and Tennessee state lines. Union forces occupied the town for much of the Civil War and established a hospital and refugee camp there. African American freedmen constructed extensive fortifications around the town and along the nearby rail lines.

From the accompanying article: "Stevenson is the junction of the Memphis and Charleston, and the Nashville and Chattanooga railroads, and is therefore a strategic position of considerable importance. . . . In the event of any attempt being made by the Southern rebels to regain possession of Tennessee, Stevenson would be one of the first places attacked. . . . On the same page we illustrate the Erection Of Stockades For Defense By Negroes. Under the new Act of Congress all negroes who come into our lines are set to work at once on fortifications, and paid wages and freed as a reward for their labor."

The War in Alabama—Fort Grant, One of the Rebel Works Protecting the Approach of Mobile
Frank Leslie's Illustrated Newspaper, October 24, 1863
Artist: E. B. Hough

In December 1862, Confederate forces constructed Fort Grant on a small island at the mouth of Mobile Bay. The fort survived two bombardments before Union vessels captured Mobile Bay in August 1864.

From the accompanying article: "The bay of Mobile, of which we give an accurate map this week, is soon to become a theatre of active operations. It is almost closed in by islands, Forts Morgan and Gaines commanding the approach to Mobile by the main channel. To protect it still better, the rebels have erected a fort near Grant's pass, of which we give a very picturesque view."

Stevenson, Alabama
Harper's Weekly, December 12, 1863
Artist: Mr. Davis

In the late 1860s, *Harper's* published *Harper's Pictorial History of the Civil War,* a compendium of engravings from the magazine. This image was reprinted in the *Pictorial History.*

From the accompanying article (in *Harper's Weekly*): "The town is unlike Bridgeport, as it has houses in it; so that one does not domicile under the railroad platform, but in a hotel; and such a hotel! The room that one sleeps in has crowded into it every mortal that it can by any possibility be made to contain, besides divers, other inhabitants of an enlivening nature."

Huntsville, Alabama, from General Logan's Head-Quarters
Harper's Weekly, March 19, 1864
Artist: unknown

In this engraving, the artist depicts Huntsville under Federal occupation.

From the accompanying article: "'This town, which is now the head-quarters of General Logan . . . is the only one in the South that I have visited,' says our correspondent, 'that in itself suggests inhabitants of cultivated taste and refinement. The streets are regularly laid out, and well shaded by fine trees. The houses, too, have architectural design—a something that few homes of "ye Tchivalrie" can boast—and have about them gardens well laid out, and very neatly kept. The inhabitants are disposed to be "Union," but are fearful of the consequence of an avowal in its favor, in event of the reoccupation of the town by the rebel troops. Still there are among the citizens very many stanch Union men, who do not hesitate to say their thought. I have seen but one female endeavor to show her dislike for the "wretched Yank." This one, after much effort, got up such a visage that I produced sketch-book and pencil to reproduce the novelty; but she would not stay en pose, and for consequence has not the distinguished honor of an appearance in Harper.'"

OUR FLEET OFF MOBILE.

VIEW OF MOBILE ALA.

Grant's Pass.

Fort Morgan.

Our Fleet off Mobile
View of Mobile, AL.
Grant's Pass
Fort Morgan
Harper's Weekly, March 26, 1864
Artist: unknown

Correspondents and artists from illustrated newspapers were generally Northern and traveled with the Union army and navy. Like American correspondents during later wars who reported conflicts from the perspective of American forces and their allies, these writers and illustrators were sympathetic to the North. To them, Alabama was a foreign battlefield and Confederate forces, the enemy. This perspective is reflected in illustrations like these, where the Confederate fortifications and the city of Mobile are seen from a distance.

From the accompanying article: "We give . . . an illustration showing the position of the Federal fleet off the harbor of Mobile, together with the defenses of the harbor. At last accounts . . . Admiral Farragut was bombarding Fort Powell, which commands Grant's Pass, on the left of the picture. This fort is bomb-proof, but, under the vigorous fire directed against it, could not, it was believed at the date of the latest advices, long hold out. The reduction of this fort is necessary to enable Farragut to send his mosquito fleet through the Pass into the harbor of Mobile, by which he will cut off forts Gaines and Morgan. . . . Mobile is one of the largest cities on the Gulf, and is fairly environed by defenses thrown up during the last two years. The authorities, however, do not appear to feel secure against assault; for . . . the Mayor of the city issued a proclamation requesting all non-combatants to leave the city, intimating that its capture was not impossible, and that in any case, if the city should be besieged, suffering might result from the want of supplies."

Soldiers' Ball at Huntsville, Alabama—Dancing the "Virginia Reel"
Harper's Weekly, April 9, 1864
Artist: unknown

This scene of Union soldiers dancing the Virginia reel with Southern women is appealing from a social perspective, depicting soldiers enjoying a respite from battle. But this illustration is artistically appealing as well. The artist's use of *chiaroscuro*—a bold contrast between light and dark—creates a pleasingly balanced scheme. The women's skirts are bright and voluminous against the backdrop of the men's dark uniforms, inserting femininity into what might otherwise look like a rigid battle line down the center of the drawing. Light pours in from an unseen window, highlighting the walls and the floor and creating a sense of warm space between men and women. The use of warm light and the softness of the scene humanizes the soldiers, who otherwise tend to look rigid and uniform. Illustrators working in black and white tend to use intense chiaroscuro. Without color, the contrasting darks and lights make an intense impact.

From the accompanying article: "The view on page 236 of a ball of the non-commissioned, officers and privates of the Fifteenth Corps at Huntsville, Alabama, is thus described by Mr. Davis, who furnishes the sketch: 'Since the occupation of this place by General Logan the soldiers have made many friends, and a few evenings since they gave a ball, at which a considerable number of ladies were present. The ball was as well conducted and as full of enjoyment as any affair of the kind ever given in this place. The soldiers, with their well-brushed though somewhat worn uniforms, clean white gloves, and bronzed, happy faces, presented a sight well worth seeing. Their very intimate acquaintance with balls of a far different nature and missions seemed to have peculiarly prepared them for enjoying such a gathering.'"

Obstructions.   Gaines.   Morgan.   Ram Tennessee.   Selma.   Steamer Nicholas.   Mobile Point Light.   Fort Morgan.

FORT MORGAN AND THE REBEL FLEET.

Fort Morgan and the Rebel Fleet
Off Mobile—Shelling a Blockade Runner
Harper's Weekly, August 20, 1864
Artist: unknown

By August 1864, Mobile Bay was one of only three Southern ports still under Confederate control. On August 5, Union naval forces commanded by Admiral David Farragut attacked with 18 ships. Once Farragut maneuvered through the mines in the harbor, his fleet overwhelmed the Confederate flotilla of four ships. Over the next three weeks, Union naval and ground forces captured the forts defending the bay, but they did not occupy the city.

From the accompanying article: "Now that Farragut's fleet has attacked Mobile, the illustrations which we furnish of the blockade off that port and of the rebel fleet must prove doubly interesting to our readers. Fort Morgan is the principal defense of the city, at the entrance of Mobile Bay. The city itself is thirty miles distant, even after forts Morgan and Gaines have been passed. Fort Morgan is so completely embanked with earthworks that only the ramparts are visible. At the left of one of the sketches may be seen the piles which obstruct the main passage into the bay. The lower sketch represents the *Metacomet,* the *Monongahela,* and the *Seminole* shelling a blockade-runner, supposed to be the *Dubeigh,* which ran aground while trying lately to get out to sea."

The Federal Army Crossing the Coosa River, Ala., on its Return from the Pursuit of the Confederates under Hood
Frank Leslie's Illustrated Newspaper, December 12, 1864
Artist: unknown, from a sketch by Stanley Fox

In December of 1864, Union general Sherman's army moved north to follow Confederate general Hood's army into Tennessee. This issue of *Frank Leslie's Illustrated Newspaper* provides a brief description of this illustration, but an adjacent article in the same issue indicates the weary state of the Confederate troops. Confederate leaders had recently met at Richmond to determine what to do about their ever-decreasing supply of white soldiers, deciding to "draft" black slaves to regain strength in their ranks. This image was reprinted at least twice and was included in *Leslie's* 1893 book *The Soldier in Our Civil War.*

From the adjacent article: "This exhibit of less than forty thousand able bodied white exempts in 'the Confederacy' east of the Mississippi River, explains the agitation of the scheme at Richmond for a draft upon the negro cabins of 'Confederate' slave-holders, to fill up the ranks of the rebel armies. The white element of the States, or rather parts of States still within the control of Davis, is exhausted."

Alabamians Receiving Rations
Harper's Weekly, August 11, 1866
Artist: A. R. Waud

This illustration portrays the work of the Bureau of Refugees, Freedmen, and Abandoned Lands (known as the Freedman's Bureau), which was created in March 1865 by President Lincoln. Though established to assist former slaves, the Bureau also aided poor southern whites who had lost family members, crops, and livestock during the war. In a sad irony, north Alabama, the area of the state most opposed to secession, suffered the most destruction from the war.

From the accompanying article: "When this sketch was made in June last, more than 20,000 of the people of Alabama—whites—were receiving Government rations; and it is believed that 10,000 more were probably sharers in the supplies thus drawn. . . . The much-abused Freedmen's Bureau has succeeded in persuading the negroes to go to work; so that they no longer look to the Government for support. . . . With the whites the case is different; the curse of laziness, which the presence of slavery inflicted upon them, is hard to overcome . . . they are almost entirely without ambition beyond the simplest wants of nature. They are, however, generally engaged in cultivating land to a limited extent, and the crops secured, the Government will withdraw its support and leave them to their own resources."

Pictures of the South—Magnolia Grove, on the Shell Road at Mobile, Alabama
Harper's Weekly, September 8, 1866
Artist: A. R. Waud

Constructed in the 1850s, Shell Road connected Mobile and Spring Hill, a fashionable nineteenth-century neighborhood. The romantic image shown in this engraving conflicts with the tone of the accompanying article, even though the text was written by the artist of the engraving. Sometimes the images of Alabama published in illustrated newspapers were more positive than the articles they accompanied.

From the accompanying article: "This city is so thoroughly uninteresting that your artist made but one sketch there. That was the picture of the Magnolia Avenue on the Shell Road—or rather what is left of it, for many of the finest trees were cut down in getting rand for the guns which were to defend the city—a needless destruction, as they never fired a shot. . . . Mobile was a terribly demoralized city during the war, and it is not to be wondered at. Garrisoned by a large force, which was entirely without occupation till toward the close of the war, such looseness pervaded its society as to make it the subject of repeated strictures in the rebel newspapers."

An Illegal Still in Alabama
Harper's Weekly, March 2, 1867
Artist: A. R. Waud

Artists for illustrated newspapers sometimes submitted random scenes, such as this image and the one following, which did not accompany lengthy articles.

From the accompanying article: "It being generally imagined that whisky is one of the necessaries of life, it could hardly be expected that the chivalric native of the South should deprive himself of the inebriating fluid. Now to buy whisky that has paid a profit to half a dozen dealers is more expensive than brewing it. Then the aforesaid native has a constitutional objective to government taxes, and a large one is gathered from the sale of spirits. Hence the still carries on contraband distillation in many a quiet nook of the Southern States."

A.R.W.

View of the Tombigbee River, Alabama
Harper's Weekly, March 2, 1867
Artist: A. R. Waud

Alfred Rudolph Waud, the artist who sketched this image and several others in the book, was born in England and trained there as an artist before moving to the United States in 1850. During the Civil War, he produced battlefield sketches for the *New York Illustrated News* and *Harper's Weekly*.

The Tombigbee River originates in Mississippi and flows through the western Alabama Black Belt. A little more than 500 miles long, the Tombigbee merges with the Alabama River to form the Mobile, which then flows into Mobile Bay. The accompanying article does not mention this image.

Emerson College, Mobile, Alabama
Harper's Weekly, October 3, 1868
Artist: unknown

Mobile's white elite opposed efforts to educate the children of freed slaves. In 1867, the military governor of Mobile arranged for the American Missionary Association to purchase a school building for black children and call the facility Emerson Institute. The school was a source of pride in the African American community, and its teachers and administrators were leaders in the fight for black political gains. The school was burned in the 1870s, reportedly by whites angered by articles from the school's newspaper.

From the accompanying article: "When the North gave freedom to the slaves of the South it saw the necessity of giving them also the education which was necessary to their proper appreciation and employment of their liberty. . . . The slaves, alive to the fact that they could learn to read openly instead of by stealth, proved most earnest and anxious students; and the good work progressed so favorably and vigorously that, in spite of the violence of old slave holders and their more rabid dupes, the poor Whites, there were in existence at the South on December 31, 1867, 3084 schools, with 6492 teachers and 189,517 pupils. . . . The school building at Mobile occupies one of the finest sites in the city, and is really one of the most substantial and commodious buildings in the State. It will furnish school-rooms for 800 pupils."

Approach to Montgomery, Alabama
Harper's Weekly, October 29, 1870
Artist: A. R. Waud

Here artist A. R. Waud gives readers a pastoral view of Montgomery and the Alabama River.

From the accompanying article: "This city is on the Alabama River, and, from its central position, was first selected by the Southern people as the capital of the seceded States. It is a place of considerable importance in the cotton trade, large amounts being shipped down the river to Mobile. The Capitol building occupies a commanding site, as is conspicuous from the surrounding country. The streets are wide and dusty, suggestive of the least interesting portions of Washington. High banks rise on both sides of the river, cut into picturesque gullies, or stretching like a wall for miles, adown which the cotton bales are pitched to the steamers below, as well as the cord-wood required to feed the furnaces."

A Night Drill on the Levee at Mobile, Alabama
Harper's Weekly, May 12, 1883
Artist: T. de Thulstrup from a sketch by J. O. Davidson

Artists for illustrated newspapers seldom completed drawings in the field. They would often make crude preliminary sketches and fill in the details later from notes or memory. This engraving, which shows an impressive use of light and shading, was made by T. de Thulstrup from a sketch by J. O. Davidson. A prolific artist and illustrator for *Harper's,* Davidson was born in Cumberland, Maryland, around 1853 and was best known for his illustrations of the sea—and particularly of Civil War naval action—created through firsthand observations and secondhand accounts.

From the accompanying article: "Any one visiting the levee at Mobile will almost any night witness the scene, a sketch of which I send you. Here the companies are drilled in various maneuvers requiring larger space than their armory affords; here also they get accustomed to drilling before a crowd of onlookers. The moving bodies of men, the flaming torches, far-reaching rays of powerful lamps through which the companies pass, now brilliantly lighted, now in deep or half shadow, the loud commands, clouds of dust, and dark background of shifting crowd, lofty shipping, and star-lit sky, make it a scene very warlike and picturesque."

Mobile—The Gulf City
Harper's Weekly, February 2, 1884
Artist: J. O. Davidson

This image, drawn from "the tower of Central Police Station," shows downtown Mobile. The tallest structure visible is the spire of Christ Episcopal Church. Unlike the earlier *Harper's* writer who found Mobile "thoroughly uninteresting," T. C. De Leon, author of the lengthy and flowery article accompanying this illustration, described the city as "picturesque." He writes, "Over all the river and bay hangs the blue-gray haze of this peculiar climate, touching the further shore with Italian tints that fade seaward into ocean blue, and leave a *dolce far niente* tone even on the picture of work day life."

From the accompanying article: "The majority of Northern readers, if they hear the name of Mobile at all, associate it with vague ideas of an inland town, or, at best, as a station en route to New Orleans, and famed for nothing in particular. Corrected by that minority whom business or pleasuring has brought within her gates, or by that smaller one which read the history of its own country, the Gulf City looms up as suddenly as surprisingly into the second city of its section in commercial importance, and as second to none in all those social aspects comprise, for want of some term more definitive, in the cant phrase 'Southern Life.'"

Szene nahe Leeds, Alabama, wahrend des Sturmes am 19, Februar 1884
Frank Leslie's Illustrated Newspaper, March 1, 1884
Artist: unknown

On February 19, 1884, storms swept across the Southeast, destroying buildings, washing away bridges, and killing dozens of people from Louisiana to Virginia. In Alabama, the most severe storm struck in the middle of the night near Leeds. There, several houses were destroyed, and at least five people were killed. The image on the left and the one on the next page come from the German language edition of *Frank Leslie's.* Although many nineteenth-century illustrations show people in static poses or show the aftermath of an event, this image, with debris flying through the air, depicts the storm in full force. Images such as this, which were often found in *Frank Leslie's* newspapers, anticipate film and video news reporting of a later age.

From the accompanying article (in the English language edition): "Portions of the Southern and Western States seem to be periodically visited with terrible tornadoes or cyclones, such as are happily unknown in other sections of the country. The latest, and probably the most destructive of them all, swept over South Carolina and Eastern Alabama.... The disaster has been an overwhelming one, surpassing all the numerous tornadoes which have visited this part of the South from year to year."

Berherung des Sturmes in Alabama
("In the Track of the Southern Cyclone" in the English language edition)
Frank Leslie's Illustrated Newspaper, March 8, 1884
Artist: unknown

This illustration depicts a view of the February storm's aftermath, published one week after the preceding image.

From the accompanying article (in the English language edition): "Our illustration 'In the Track of the Southern Cyclone' shows with striking vividness the terrible effects of the storm which swept over four States week before last. No more destructive cyclone has ever visited that section, where thousands of the survivors of its violence are now charges upon the public bounty, having lost everything they possessed. The number of lives lost is not yet known . . . while the loss of property mounts into the millions. Death, destruction, destitution and suffering mark the track of the storm everywhere."

THE CAMP GROUND.—Drawn by Louis Joutel.

CAPTAIN TOM SCURRY.
Photographed by C. J. Wright,
Houston, Texas.

THE GRAND REVIEW.—Drawn by Schell and Hogan.

The Camp Ground
The Grand Review
The Prize Company
Harper's Weekly, May 23, 1885
Artists: Louis Joutrl, Schell and Hogan from drawings by Horace Bradley

Harper's often featured engravings of military drills, a popular form of entertainment in the nineteenth century.

From the accompanying article: "The competitive drill of companies of militia at Mobile, Alabama, May 6-9, was noteworthy not only by reason of the splendid spectacles it presented, but by reason also of the number of companies that participated, the number of States, Western and Southern, from which they came, and the presence of many distinguished visitors. . . . The bright uniforms, blue and gray, with a great variety of decorations . . . the pleasant association in the common camp of veterans of either army in the civil war and of younger companies which have inherited the war stories of either side; the pleasant early summer weather on the Gulf coast (in spite of one day of unpleasant heat); the intense local interest taken in the contest by the citizens of every city from which companies went; the popular enthusiasm which the characteristic Southern love of military display aroused; the drilling of more than a thousand picked men from eleven States; and the presence of ladies and distinguished visitors from every one of those States—these gave the hospitable city of Mobile a week of unusual gayety."

The New Bridge over the Alabama at Selma
Harper's Weekly, July 25, 1885
Artist: unknown

Harper's celebrated the construction of a footbridge for wagons and pedestrians at Selma as a sign of progress in the industrializing post–Civil War South.

From the accompanying article: "The first bridge (except railroad bridges) ever built across the Alabama River for two hundred miles from its mouth is the iron bridge at Selma which was formally opened some two months ago. Its formal opening was properly celebrated as an achievement of the new spirit of material development that is making such notable changes in the Southern States. The business houses of Selma were closed, and 'Bridge Day' was a holiday. The citizens, including the school-children, and the citizens and military companies of the adjacent towns, formed a procession, the town was decorated, and illuminated at night, and all that oratory, poetry, and fire-works could do was done to make the day memorable in local history. . . . The lack of bridges upon even the most important and frequented highways was one of the commonest sources of surprise and complaint among travelers through the South in the old days before the war."

Alabama—Fiftieth Anniversary of the Montgomery True Blues—A Historic Organization and its Officers
Frank Leslie's Illustrated Newspaper, March 13, 1886
Artist: unknown

The Montgomery True Blues were organized in 1836 to fight in the Seminole War. The company volunteered for service in the Mexican War of 1846 but traveled only as far as Mobile before being informed that no more troops were needed. The Blues returned home. During the Civil War, the Blues served as an artillery unit in the Confederate army and later, in the 1870s, reorganized as a unit of the state militia. The Blues took part in the interstate drill previously pictured.

From the accompanying article: "Among the attractions at the recent celebration of the fiftieth anniversary of the organization of the company, was the presentation, by the ladies of Montgomery, of a beautiful silk flag. . . . Among the guests of the occasion was a veteran of the Seminole War. . . . In this bright old company's record of war and peace the whole country will justly feel a pride. The Blues entertain almost daily at their handsome company rooms."

Alabama—The Recent Floods in the Alabama River—A Family Refuge in a Tree-Top
Frank Leslie's Illustrated Newspaper, April 17, 1886
Artist: unknown, from a sketch by R. A. Templeton

This image of an African American woman shows a striking evolution in the portrayal of blacks in illustrated newspapers. Although many images of the time show blacks, Jews, people of Irish descent, and others as grotesque caricatures, this representation presents an attractive woman with natural features.

From the accompanying article: "The 'Spring freshets' began their destructive outbreak with remarkable unanimity at the opening of the showery month. . . . With the great storm of March 29th began the overflow of the Alabama, Warrior, Coosa, Tallapoosa, Cumberland, Tombigbee and Cahaba Rivers, together with their numerous tributaries. By April 1st, hundreds of miles of territory in East and Middle Tennessee, North Georgia and North Alabama were under water. Alabama suffered most. Plantations were inundated, houses and mills swept away, with thousands of horses, mules, cattle and hogs. . . . Steamboat men on the Alabama River reported on Monday of last week that every plantation for three hundred miles around, from ten miles up river from Mobile, was under water. . . . These lowlands are mostly inhabited by negroes, who, being more or less accustomed to such floods, were generally provided with skills or bateaux, and were enabled to save some of their live stock by removing them to platforms erected above the water."

Birmingham, Alabama—Scene in a Real Estate Exchange
Harper's Weekly, March 26, 1887
Artist: John Durkin

In 1887, *Harper's* ran supplements containing a series of feature articles and images on cities of "the Industrial South." Cities highlighted included Richmond, Atlanta, and Birmingham. This image and the three that follow come from that supplement.

From the accompanying article: "The most remarkable features of the place have been, and are still, the rapid appreciation in value of city and suburban real estate, and the hourly increase in magnitude and volume of the transactions in this line of business. Sales take place daily in the office of the Elyton Land Company, which continues to exercise a controlling influence upon all the real estate transfers of the city, and when its doors are opened the eagerness with which the throngs of buyers crowd about the large maps indicating the property to be sold recalls the palmy days of the New York Gold Board or the San Francisco Stock Exchange. Prices which a few years or even months ago would have seemed fabulous are freely offered and given. A purchaser hardly concludes his bargain before he perceives an opportunity to sell at a handsome profit, so that the same piece of land frequently changes hands several times in the course of a day, and at sunset is valued at thousands of dollars more than it was in the morning."

The Great Industry of Birmingham, Alabama—A Pig Iron Furnace
Harper's Weekly, March 26, 1887
Artist: Charles Graham

Producing iron in a casting shed like the one shown here was difficult and dangerous work. When the blast furnace was "tapped," workers removed a plug and released molten iron that exploded into trenches and then flowed into smaller channels called sows. The red hot iron threw showers of sparks, and workers were often burned. Wearing special shoes with oversized wooden soles, the workers guided the liquid iron into still smaller channels called pigs. As the iron cooled and turned solid, it was covered with sand and later sprayed with water. Once solid, the heavy iron bars, also called pigs, were broken off and loaded onto wagons.

From the accompanying article: "On November 23, 1880, 'Alice' furnace, the first erected within the city limits, went into blast, and produced an excellent quality of pig iron from ore, coke, and limestone procured from its immediate vicinity. The cost of this production was comparatively so small as to be surprising and from that date Birmingham's future as a great iron producing and manufacturing centre was assured. The inhabitants of the city suddenly awoke to the fact that its fortunes were advancing upon the crest of a tidal wave of prosperity, and they hastened to take advantage of this happy condition of affairs. Furnace after furnace was erected, new mines were opened on every side, foundries, machine shops, and various iron manufactories sprang into a sudden existence, and railroads were built toward the city so rapidly from all directions that today six trunk lines, possessing innumerable branches, are in operation and speeding their trains into its handsome new Union Depot."

Charcoal Burners
Harper's Weekly, March 26, 1887
Artist: Horace Bradley

Birmingham's industry required large amounts of charcoal, produced by burning wood. Charcoal was used in blast furnaces as well as in manufacturing works and blacksmith shops. Pine trees, abundant in the Birmingham area, produced good-quality charcoal.

The artist who drew this image, Horace James Bradley, served as an art editor and illustrator for *Harper's Weekly* from 1886 until he died of tuberculosis in 1896 at age 34. He was a founding member and later president and director of New York Art Students League, a school that thrives today on West 57th Street in Manhattan, having helped to train artists such as Norman Rockwell, Georgia O'Keeffe, and Jackson Pollock.

Coke Ovens
Harper's Weekly, March 26, 1887
Artist: Horace Bradley

Beehive ovens such as those shown here were used to heat coal to more than 2,000 degrees to produce an industrial product called coke. In a blast furnace, coke burns hotter and is more efficient for making iron. The article does not provide the exact location for these ovens, but by the time this engraving was published, coke ovens were operated at various locations in the Birmingham area, including Sloss Furnaces and Coalburg. One year after this engraving, 100 new ovens were constructed at Brookside. One part of the area that became Pratt City was known in the 1890s as Coketown.

Wharf Scene at Mobile, Alabama
Harper's Weekly, July 16, 1887
Artist: Charles Graham

The Northern press celebrated the economic possibilities of the industrial New South. This illustration features a bustling port in Mobile, jammed with ships and laden with goods waiting to be exported. The accompanying article describes Alabama's resources, including timber, iron, and the state's navigable waterways. The masthead drawing on this publication highlights the South's old and new industries—manufactures, iron, tobacco, cotton, and sugarcane—forecasting continued economic revival.

From the accompanying article: "Mobile is not dead. She has been sleeping a long sleep, visited by many troubled dreams, and from this she is barely beginning to awaken; but the full awakening is at hand, and it bids fair to precede a period of growth, business activity and prosperity hitherto undreamed of. She has been a staunch adherent of King Cotton, and her shattered fortunes are the result of his partial dethronement."

The · Capitol

Montgomery, Alabama
Harper's Weekly, July 16, 1887
Artist: Charles Graham

Charles Graham, the artist who drew this image and the one on the preceding page, was a self-taught illustrator from Rock Island, Illinois. He contributed drawings for nearly every issue of *Harper's Weekly* between 1880 and 1892. Graham traveled throughout the post–Civil War South with fellow artist Horace Bradley, drawing his favorite subject: town scenes. Here, Graham suggests genteel decadence by placing the open shutter and wrought-iron balconies in the foreground of his subject. Up Dexter Avenue (formerly Market Street) toward the Alabama state capitol is Dexter Avenue Baptist Church, visible on the right.

From the accompanying article: "The pure air, the absence of din and clatter, and the evidence of a long-established prosperity that form distinctive features of Montgomery, the capital city of Alabama, are in refreshing contrast to the smoke, noise, and feverish bustle of the more recently founded coal and iron towns of the State."

The Attack on the Jail at Birmingham, Alabama
Harper's Weekly, December 22, 1888
Artist: unknown

Birmingham resident Richard Hawes was arrested in December 1888 for the murder of his family. When a lynch mob attempted to take Hawes from the county jail on Twenty-first Street North, guards fired on the mob, killing several men. Hawes was later convicted and hanged. In this image, the building with scaffolding on the far right is the Jefferson County Courthouse, still under construction. Guards can be seen on the roof of the jail. The church beyond the jail is First Presbyterian Church.

From the accompanying article: "A crowd of men appeared at the entrance of the jail at Birmingham, Alabama, at eleven o'clock on the night of Saturday, December 8th, with the expressed intention of lynching Richard R. Hawes, a railroad engineer, who was confined there on a charge of having atrociously murdered his wife and daughter. . . .

By the time that the mob reached the jail it was two thousand strong. . . . Sheriff Smith and Chief of Police Pickard first saw the mob as it turned into an alleyway leading to the jail door. They called out to the men to stop, on pain of death. This warning was repeated several times, but the mob did not take heed. Then, as the sheriff asserts, a shot was fired by a man in the crowd. An instant later, in response to a command from the sheriff, the guards fired a volley into the thick of the mob. The effect was awful. Three men were killed outright, seven were mortally wounded, and thirty were less seriously hurt. Six of the seven mortally wounded men died within a short time. The mob dispersed, and did not renew the attack."

Alabama—Disastrous Wreck, Near Birmingham, of a Special Train Bearing German Singing Societies to the New Orleans Saengerfest
Frank Leslie's Illustrated Newspaper, March 8, 1890
Artist: unknown

In mid-February 1890, American singers of German descent traveled to New Orleans from several states to participate in the annual National Saengerfest, or "singer's festival." Groups from Chicago arrived late because their train wrecked near Birmingham. The *New York Times* described the passengers as "badly shaken up" when they arrived in New Orleans the next morning. Three required hospitalization, including one with a broken leg and one with internal injuries.

From the accompanying article: "We illustrate on page 100 the recent disaster some forty miles from Birmingham, Alabama, in which a special train bearing a number of German singing societies to the Saengerfest at New Orleans collided with an accommodation train and was totally wrecked. The engineer of the special train was instantly killed and a number of the passengers badly wounded. The wonder is that every person on the train was not killed, so complete was the smash-up."

Booker T. Washington, President of the Tuskegee Normal and Industrial School
Harper's Weekly, September 14, 1895
Artist: unknown

By the 1890s, printing technology had advanced so that newspapers could now include photographs. This portrait of Booker T. Washington, engraved from a photograph, is accompanied by a lengthy feature article on Tuskegee Institute that is illustrated with photographs. Newspapers often reused engraved portraits (sometimes using the same portrait to represent two different people), and this image depicts a likeness younger than Washington's 39 years at the time.

This issue of *Harper's* also contained a feature article and engraved illustrations highlighting the forthcoming Cotton States and International Exposition, a grand fair celebrating the industry and agriculture of the South. Washington spoke at the opening ceremonies, and his address came to be known as the Atlanta Compromise. In the speech, Washington called for better relations and cooperation between the races and acknowledged certain realities of the time, most notably racial segregation. Whites throughout the nation embraced Washington as a non-threatening "negro leader."

From the accompanying article: "This young man, not yet in middle life, went to Hampton from his Virginia home in a state of absolute poverty; but his forlorn condition did not long conceal from the teachers at Hampton that he possessed great earnestness and force, and what might appropriately be called a genius of common-sense."

Notes on the Engravings

These notes, listed by page number, attempt to include all aspects known of the engravings. Each of the engravings is identified by the page number, engraving's title or description, and catalog number from the Birmingham Public Library's archival collection. Although every attempt was made to collect all data, in some cases complete data was unavailable due to the age and condition of some of the engravings and records.

II   **The Market, Mobile**
Birmingham Public Library
Archives
1924.1.13

VIII   **The Morris Iron Mine**
Birmingham Public Library
Archives
1924.1.15

3   **The Seceding Delegation in Congress**
Birmingham Public Library
Archives
1924.1.14

4   **William R. King**
Birmingham Public Library
Archives
1924.1.43

6   **Residence of the Late Vice President King**
Birmingham Public Library
Archives
1924.1.30

8   **Scene on the Alabama River, Loading Cotton**
Birmingham Public Library
Archives
1924.1.1

10   **The Tilt**
Birmingham Public Library
Archives
1924.1.28

12   **The Amphitheater**
Birmingham Public Library
Archives
1924.1.28

14   **Montgomery State House, 1861**
Birmingham Public Library
Archives
1924.1.14

16   **Inauguration of Davis**
Birmingham Public Library
Archives
1924.1.7

18   **Cotton-Shoot on the Alabama**
Birmingham Public Library
Archives
1924.1.32

20   **Montgomery, 1861**
Birmingham Public Library
Archives
1924.1.22

22   **The Confederate Cabinet**
Birmingham Public Library
Archives
1924.1.22

24   **The White House at Montgomery, 1861**
Birmingham Public Library
Archives
1924.1.22

26   **Union Southern Men Welcoming Gunboats**
Birmingham Public Library
Archives
1924.1.17

28   **Huntsville, 1862**
Birmingham Public Library
Archives
1924.1.24

30   **Searching for Rebels**
Birmingham Public Library
Archives
1924.1.21

32   **Murder of Gen. Robert L. McCook**
Birmingham Public Library
Archives
1924.1.10

34   **Stevenson, 1862**
Birmingham Public Library
Archives
1924.1.38

36   **Fort Grant**
Birmingham Public Library
Archives
1924.1.31

38 Stevenson, 1863
Birmingham Public Library
Archives
1924.1.39

40 Huntsville from Logan's Headquarters
Birmingham Public Library
Archives
1924.1.20

42 Fleet off Mobile; View of Mobile; Grant's Pass; Fort Morgan
Birmingham Public Library
Archives
1924.1.5

44 Soldiers' Ball at Huntsville: Dancing the Virginia Reel
Birmingham Public Library
Archives
1924.1.4

46 Fort Morgan and the Rebel Fleet; Shelling a Blockade Runner
Birmingham Public Library
Archives
1924.1.27

48 Federal Army Crossing the Coosa
Birmingham Public Library
Archives
1924.1.40

50 Receiving Rations
Birmingham Public Library
Archives
1924.1.9

52 Pictures of the South—Magnolia Grove
Birmingham Public Library
Archives
1924.1.12

54 An Illegal Still
Birmingham Public Library
Archives
1924.1.25

56 Tombigbee River
Birmingham Public Library
Archives
1924.1.25

58 Emerson College,
Birmingham Public Library
Archives
1924.1.3

60 Approach to Montgomery
Birmingham Public Library
Archives
1924.1.8

62 A Night Drill on the Levee at Mobile
Birmingham Public Library
Archives
1924.1.19

64 Mobile—The Gulf City, 1884
Birmingham Public Library
Archives
1924.1.26

66 Szene nahe Leeds, Alabama, Wahrend des Sturmes
Birmingham Public Library
Archives
1924.1.36

68 Berherung des Sturmes
Birmingham Public Library
Archives
1924.1.33

70 Military Drills
Birmingham Public Library
Archives
1924.1.23

72 New Bridge, Selma
Birmingham Public Library
Archives
1924.1.16

74 Fiftieth Anniversary of The True Blues
Birmingham Public Library
Archives
1924.1.29

76 Floods in the Alabama River— Family Refuge in a Treetop
Birmingham Public Library
Archives
1924.1.37

78 Real Estate Exchange, Birmingham
Birmingham Public Library
Archives
1924.1.11

80 Pig Iron Furnace
Birmingham Public Library
Archives
1924.1.11

82 Charcoal Burners
Birmingham Public Library
Archives
1924.1.11

84 Coke Ovens
Birmingham Public Library
Archives
1924.1.11

86 Mobile Wharf
Birmingham Public Library
Archives
1924.1.13

88 Montgomery, 1887
Birmingham Public Library
Archives
1924.1.13

90 Attack on the Jail at Birmingham, 1888
Birmingham Public Library
Archives
1924.1.2

92 Train Wreck near Birmingham, 1890
Birmingham Public Library
Archives
1924.1.35

94 Booker T. Washington
Birmingham Public Library
Archives
1924.1.42

Suggestions for Additional Reading

Many Alabama engravings are still available at nominal prices from online dealers and rare book and manuscript shops. For readers wishing to learn more about the range of Alabama images published, and perhaps wishing to collect these images, the indispensable source is the annotated checklist by Joseph J. Forbes, *Views of Alabama in Nineteenth Century Illustrated Newspapers,* published in 1994 and available for purchase from the Birmingham Public Library.

For readers who wish to learn more about the subjects of these engraved images, there is a rich historical literature on Alabama. The best general history is *Alabama: The History of a Deep South State* (University of Alabama Press, 1994) by William Warren Rogers, Robert David Ward, Leah Rawls Atkins, and Wayne Flynt.

On Alabama in the antebellum period, see Thomas Perkins Abernethy's *The Formative Period in Alabama, 1815-1828* (The University of Alabama Press, 1990 reprint) and Weymouth T. Jordan's *Ante-Bellum Alabama: Town and Country* (University of Alabama Press, 1986 reprint).

Alabama in the Civil War and Reconstruction period is explored in Arthur W. Bergeron, Jr.'s *Confederate Mobile* (University Press of Mississippi, 1991); William Warren Rogers, Jr.'s *Confederate Home Front: Montgomery During the Civil War* (University of Alabama Press, 1999); Margaret M. Storey's *Loyalty and Loss: Alabama's Unionists in the Civil War and Reconstruction* (Louisiana State University Press, 2004); Dan T. Carter's *When the War Was Over: The Failure of Self-Reconstruction in the South, 1865-1867* (Louisiana State University Press, 1985); and Michael W. Fitzgerald's *Urban Emancipation: Popular Politics in Reconstruction Mobile, 1860-1890* (Louisiana State University Press, 2002).

Among the books that explore the South's image in the nineteenth century, two are especially useful: *Away Down South: A History of Southern Identity* by James C. Cobb (Oxford University Press, 2005) and Michael O'Brien's *The Idea of the American South, 1920-1941* (Johns Hopkins University Press, 1979).

Sources on illustrated newspapers and engraved illustrations include *Frank Leslie and His Illustrated Newspaper, 1855-1860* by Budd Leslie Gambee, Jr. (University of Michigan, Department of Library Science, 1964); *The South on Paper: Line, Color and Light* by Estill C. Pennington and James C. Kelly (University of South Carolina Press, 2000); and *How to Identify Prints: A Complete Guide to Manual and Mechanical Processes from Woodcuts to Inkjet* by Bamber Gascoigne (Thames and Hudson, 2004).

Readers interested to see engraved images of another place, in this case New York City, should see John Grafton's *New York in the Nineteenth Century: 321 Engravings from "Harper's Weekly" and Other Contemporary Sources* (Dover Publications, 1977).

ALABAMA ILLUSTRATED ENGRAVINGS FROM 19TH CENTURY NEWSPAPERS

In the nineteenth century, the people of Alabama relied on ewspapers to learn about the world outside their own hometowns. Prior to the 1890s, the technology did not exist to economically publish photographs in newspapers, so some publishers employed artists to draw and engrave images of places, events, and people. Many of these engraved illustrations, which accompanied news stories, poems, and short fiction, are impressive for their detail and artistic quality.

From the 1850s to the 1890s, more than 250 engraved images of Alabama were published in national and international illustrated newspapers. This book contains nearly 50 of those illustrations from five nineteenth-century newspapers such as *Harper's Weekly*. These striking black-and-white images depict city and country scenes of everything from politics and civil war to agriculture, industry, entertainment, and everyday life, providing readers passionate about history and art a unique insight into Alabama's rich cultural past.

James L. Baggett is Head of the Department of Archives and Manuscripts at the Birmingham Public Library, and Archivist for the City of Birmingham.

A past president of the Society of Alabama Archivists and past Chair of the Jefferson County Historical Commission, he is the editor of three previous books, including *A Woman of the Town: Louise Wooster, Birmingham's Magdalen*.

Kelsey Scouten Bates is Assistant Archivist and Grants Writer at the Birmingham Public Library. She is currently pursuing a Ph.D. in English at the University of Alabama and has an M.S. in Professional Writing from Towson University. She formerly taught English as a Second Language in Taiwan and worked as a grants writer at the Baltimore Museum of Art.

WWW.TURNERPUBLISHING.COM

www.ingramcontent.com/pod-product-compliance
Lightning Source LLC
Chambersburg PA
CBHW061226150426
42812CB00054BA/2528